BEYOND THE BRANCHES

Writing and Scrapping your Personal Family Tree

Robyn Conley

Roots & Branches
Denton, Texas

Published by Roots and Branches, an imprint of AWOC.COM Publishing, P.O. Box 2819, Denton, TX 76202, USA.

ISBN: 978-0-937660-24-9

Visit the the author's website: http://www.robynconley.com

Dedication

For Grandad, Dad, Mom,
Grandma, Russell, Schelle,
Rikki, Andrew and Samantha…

Thank you for helping me carry
on those family memories

Tips for using this interactive Family Tree Guide

Remembering is the key. This is the time to let your memories have full rein and play. The prompts provided are simply that. Simply "answering" them would be selling yourself short to you in this time frame and to your family members who will savor these insights of yours in their future.

So use the prompts as jump-starters for your memories. They'll trigger details you'll be surprised you remember—details that will mean the world to your children and grandchildren when they've reached the age to appreciate such things.

Sounds are important; smells are crucial; what you felt, tasted, heard and observed all need to be included in each section. This book should not read like an outline, but like someone might have jotted down after sitting in on the stories told around the family table with chicken and mashed potatoes still warm on the plates.

This is your story made up of lots of stories about you and your family, both past and present. Enjoy it and thanks for passing it along to those who would never know these things if you hadn't taken the time to play in your memory.

Note the sample "life" quotes at the end of this book. Cut them out and paste where appropriate, or come up with your own!

My Complete Family Tree History

My Name: ____

Date of Birth: ____

Place of Birth: ____

My Mother: ____

My Father: ____

My Grandparents:

My Great-grandparents:

My Great-grandparents

My Siblings:

My Aunts:

My Uncles:

My Cousins:

Military Service—who and branch:

Others relatives:

Special relatives

Special relatives I remember as a kid…
places, towns where we saw each other…
what we did together…

Journal Entries

Photos/memorabilia

Where I lived

Places where I lived as a young child
what I remember about those places…
schools, teachers, friends, where I played outside…
my favorite smells…things that made me smile…sad…

Journal Entries

Photos/memorabilia

Vacations

Favorite family vacations…
trips to camp…
where we went, what was funny or scary or disastrous:

Journal Entries

Photos/memorabilia

High School

Where I attended high school…
the campus, the town, the activities I participated in and why I chose them…
favorite friends…
teachers who inspired me…
awards I earned…

Journal Entries

Photos/memorabilia

My first crushes–kisses

who I thought I'd be interested in…
dates I went on…
proms or dances…
other special occasions…

Journal Entries

Photos/memorabilia

My first car

model, color, special details about it…
wrecks…
tickets…
day trips with friends…

Journal Entries

Photos/memorabilia

College

Where I wanted to go to college…
where I went to college
dreams I had for my career…
special training during the transition from High School to career…

Journal Entries

Photos/memorabilia

My First Job

friends, coworkers from that time…
Personal values during my young adulthood…
mistakes, lessons learned…
what my parents/family members were like then…
adventures I had when I was a single person…

Journal Entries

Photos/memorabilia

Falling In Love

courtship moments, memories…
wedding planning/mishaps/ceremony…

Journal Entries

Photos/memorabilia

Early Marriage Years

first "home" details (inside/outside)
friends we enjoyed…
cars we had…
pets we had…
trials and joys…

Journal Entries

Photos/memorabilia

Starting a Family

pregnancy moments/cravings/showers and other memories…
nursery details…
worries or wonderings about being a new parent…
grandparents…what were they like?
the birth…

Journal Entries

Photos/memorabilia

The Crazy/Busy Years of Young Parenthood

toddler memories…
first school adventures…
memories of favorite times with grandparents…
other home details…
insights to offer about finances, lessons learned…

Journal Entries

Photos/memorabilia

Vacations/Trips As a Young Family…

means of travel, places visited…
people we met, favorite/funny memories…

Journal Entries

Photos/memorabilia

Career Highlights

favorite jobs…
interesting business trips…
achievements, awards, special projects I was proud of…

Journal Entries

Photos/memorabilia

Times of Growth

emotional trials…
caring for aging parents…
blessings in the painful moments…

Journal Entries

Photos/memorabilia

Where My Relatives Are Now

people I miss…
what I'd like to let my family know about my spirit…

Journal Entries

Photos/memorabilia

Quotes about life:

"But men must know, that in this theatre of man's life it is reserved only for God and angels to be lookers on."
—Francis Bacon

"Living is my job and my art."
—Montaigne

"Only a life lived for others is the life worth while."
—Albert Einstein

"We are always getting ready to live, but never living."
—Ralph Waldo Emerson

"Were it offered to my choice, I should have no objection to a repetition of the same life from its beginning, only asking the advantages authors have in a second edition to correct some faults of the first."
—Benjamin Franklin

"Without discipline, there's no life at all."
—Katherine Hepburn

"Life is a romantic business. It is painting a picture, not doing a sum."
—Oliver Wendell Holmes, Jr.

"Life's a voyage that's homeward bound."
—Herman Melville

"Let us endeavor so to live that when we come to die even the undertaker will be sorry."
—Mark Twain

"You know, we're kicking our way into adolescence from the minute we're born. Gradually you form your own ideas of how you should lead your life…"
—Ernest Hemingway

"That it will never come again is what makes life so sweet."
—Emily Dickinson

"We sleep, but the loom of life never stops and the pattern which was weaving when the sun went down is weaving when it comes up tomorrow."
—Henry Ward Beecher

"Thanks in old age—thanks ere I go,
For health, the midday sun, the impalpable air—for life, mere life."
—Walt Whitman

"All my life I used to wonder what I would become when I grew up. Then, about seven years ago, I realized that I was never going to grow up…that growing is an ever ongoing process."
—M. Scott Peck

"It's never too late to be what you might have been."
—George Eliot

"Three grand essentials to happiness in this life are something to do, something to love, and something to hope for."
—Joseph Addison

Printed in the United States
69393LVS00003B/47-52

9 780937 660249